80⁺ Cross-Stitc
KIND THOUC

Kooler Design Studio's award winning designers, Barbara Baatz Hillman, Linda Gillum, Sandy Orton, and Donna Yuen, have collaborated to bring you 80+ clever, little, thought provoking cross stitch designs. Each has a kind saying that is the ideal sentiment for someone you know who would appreciate a gift made by you just for them.

Whether you are looking for cute, funny, serious or inspirational, you will find the perfect design for the perfect reason. Each and every design is unique and can be stitched on shirts, bags, pillows, towels and more. Why not add a few to your scrapbook pages for that extra special touch? From the moment you begin, this collection of kind thoughts will soon become your favorite cross-stitch book.

KOOLER DESIGN STUDIO BOOKS

Produced By: Kooler Design Studio
399 Taylor Blvd., Ste. 104, Pleasant Hill, CA 94523
www.koolerdesign.com

Creative Director, Donna Kooler
Editor-in-Chief, Judy Swager
Technical Editor, Priscilla Timm
Graphic Designer, María Parrish
Proofreader, Virginia Hanley-Rivett

LEISURE ARTS®
the art of everyday living

PRINTED WITH SOY INK

Made in U.S.A.

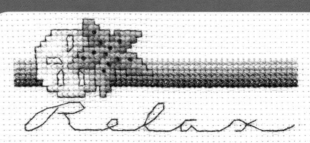

Charts are in numerical order beginning on page 5.

Back Cover

Front Cover

80+ Cross-Stitch
KIND THOUGHTS

By
Kooler
Design
Studio

#3995   U.S $9.95

0 28906 03995 5
Made in U.S.A

Page 2

Page 3

Full & Quarter Stitches ① 1. 44w X 44h

x	1/4	Back	FK	DMC	Anc.
⊙	⊡			1	2
■	■	✎		310	403
♥		✎		666	46
m	m			743	302
⚓	↓			826	161
?	?			977	1002
T	T			3755	140
⊠	⊠			3776	1048
		✎	⊙	3837	111

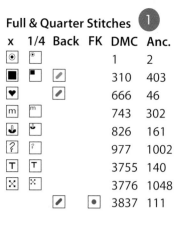

43w X 52h

Full & Quarter Stitches ②

x	1/4	Back	FK	DMC	Anc.
◗				210	108
		✎		317	400
♥				350	11
∩		✎		741	304
I				744	301
		✎	⊙	824	164
◆				826	161
■				913	204
m				964	185
‡				3326	36

5

3. 49w X 64h

3

Full & Quarter Stitches

x	1/4	Back	FK	DMC	Anc.
⊙	⊡			1	2
+	+			210	108
■	◪		✎	310	403
			✎	312	979
♥				350	11
A	A			353	6
⊥	⊥			436	1045
∿	∿			744	301
◪	◪	⊙		776	24
♠	♠			798	131
⊠	⊠		✎	801	359
★	★	⊙		809	130
H	H			818	23
n	n			842	388
◧	◧			955	206
✿				959	186
⊠	⊠			3841	128

Full & Quarter Stitches

4

x	1/4	Back	FK	Ply	DMC	Anc.
⊙	⊡			2	1	2
◪				2	155	109
◆		✎		2	333	119
			⊙	1	333	119
m					341	117
♠	♠			2	415	398
I	I			2	762	234
H	H			2	3747	120
♠				2	3853	1003
A				2	3854	1047

4. 53w X 20h

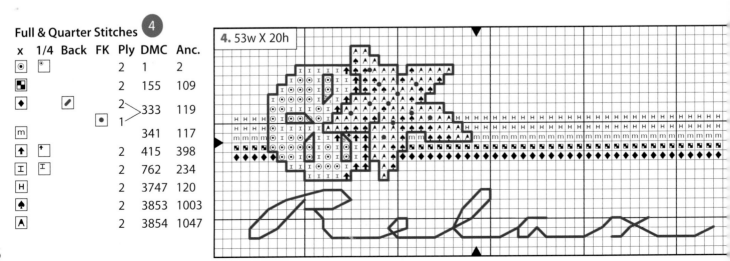

5. 50w X 50h

7. 17w X 42h

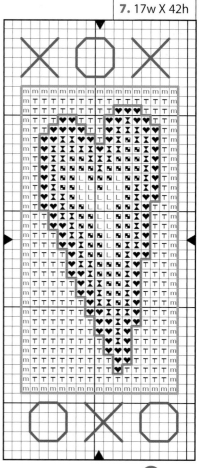

6. 22w X 38h

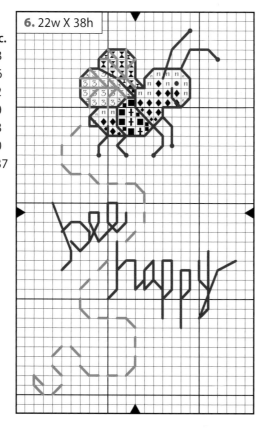

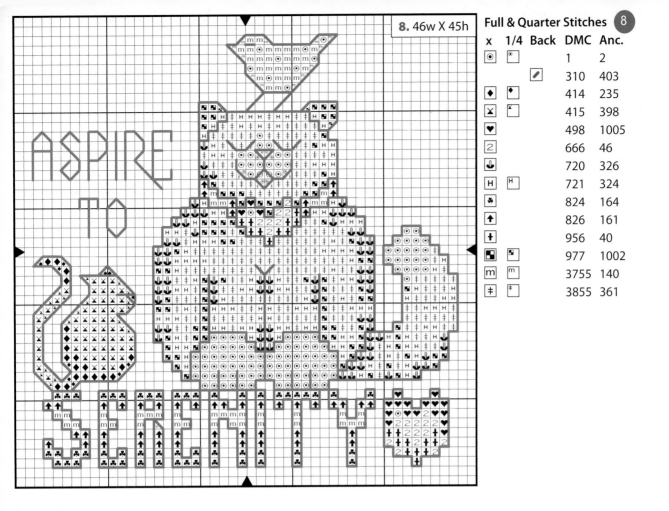

Full & Quarter Stitches 8

x	1/4	Back	DMC	Anc.
⊙	⊙		1	2
		✎	310	403
◆	◆		414	235
✕	✕		415	398
♥			498	1005
2			666	46
⚓			720	326
H	H		721	324
♣			824	164
↑			826	161
✝			956	40
◪	◪		977	1002
m	m		3755	140
‡	‡		3855	361

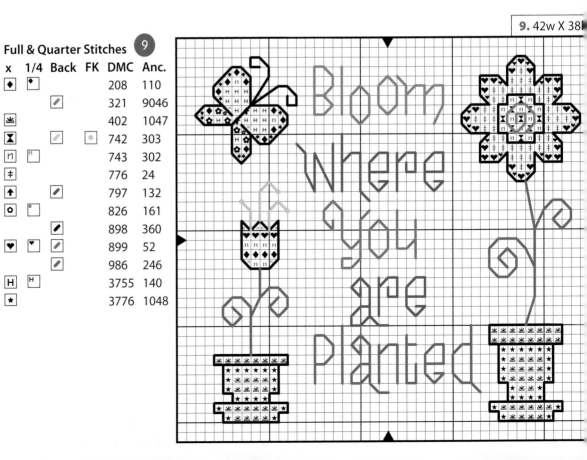

Full & Quarter Stitches 9

x	1/4	Back	FK	DMC	Anc.
◆	◆			208	110
		✎		321	9046
⚘				402	1047
✕		✎	⦿	742	303
n	n			743	302
‡				776	24
↑		✎		797	132
○	°			826	161
		✎		898	360
♥	♥	✎		899	52
		✎		986	246
H	H			3755	140
★				3776	1048

Full & Quarter Stitches 10

x	1/4	Back	FK	DMC	Anc.
⊙	⊙			1	2
■	■		●	310	403
✝	✝		●	414	235
+	+			415	398
▫	▫			434	310
~	~			436	1045
✗	✗			721	324
‡	‡			722	323
T	T			739	387
◆	◆			839	360
◒	◒			841	378
		✎	●	898	360
↑	↑			920	1004

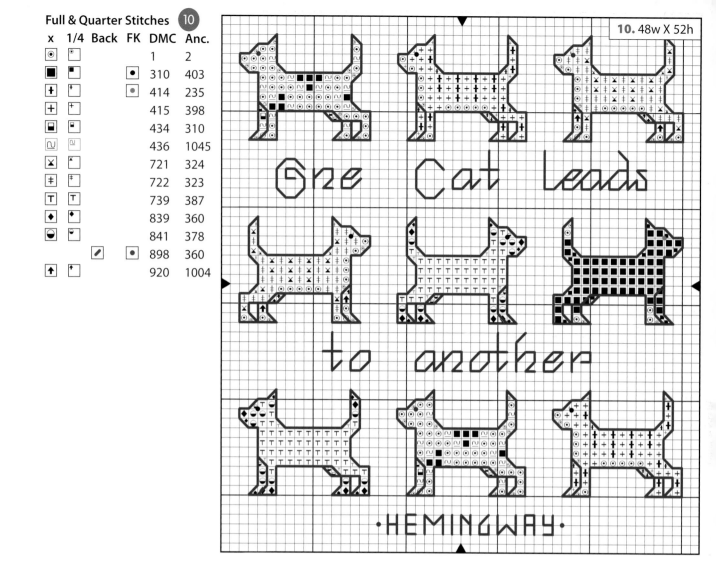

One Cat Leads to another ·HEMINGWAY·

is the art of GOD ·DANTE·

52w X 38h

Full & Quarter Stitches 11

x	1/4	Back	FK	DMC	Anc.
○				156	117
✗				210	108
☆				211	342
		✎	●	312	979
◆				341	117
		✎		501	878
↑				502	877
⊠				742	303
▫				743	302
H				744	301
m	m			954	203
T	T			955	206
n				3747	120

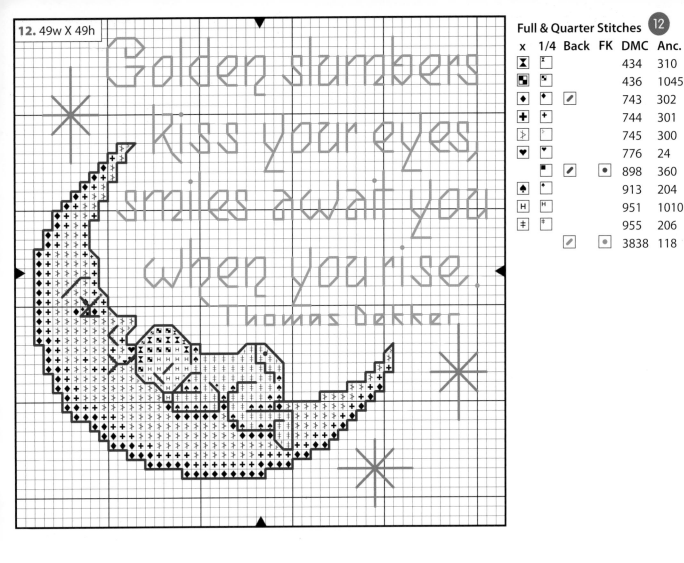

12. 49w X 49h

Full & Quarter Stitches 12

x	1/4	Back	FK	DMC	Anc.
⊠	⊡			434	310
▣	◪			436	1045
◆	◆	✎		743	302
✚	✚			744	301
⊅	⊅			745	300
♥	♥			776	24
▣	◪	✎	●	898	360
♠	♠			913	204
H	H			951	1010
‡	‡			955	206
		✎	●	3838	118

Full & Quarter Stitches 13

x	1/4	Back	FK	DMC	Anc.
⚓				208	110
◆	◆			334	977
♥	♥			349	13
✗	✗			350	11
●	●			434	310
✚	✚			436	1045
‡				704	256
◗	◗			722	323
▣	◪	✎		742	303
m	m			744	301
✲				775	128
		✎	●	898	360
♣	♣			911	205
⬥				913	204
▣				3325	129

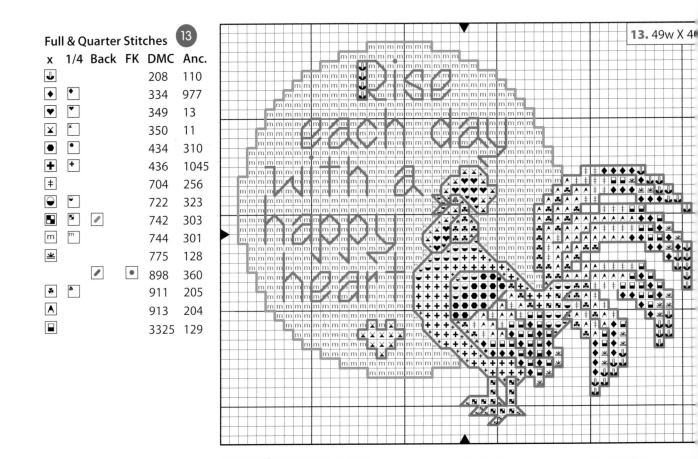

13. 49w X 4█

10

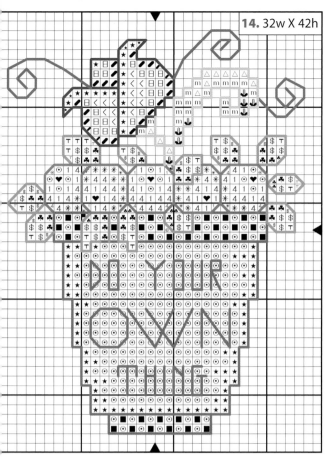

14. 32w X 42h

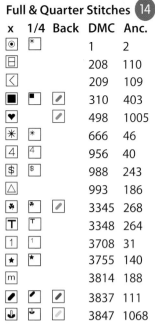

Full & Quarter Stitches 14

x	1/4	Back	DMC	Anc.
⊙	⊙		1	2
⊟			208	110
<			209	109
■	■	/	310	403
♥		/	498	1005
✳	✳		666	46
4	4		956	40
$	$		988	243
△			993	186
♣	♣	/	3345	268
T	T		3348	264
1	1		3708	31
★	★		3755	140
m			3814	188
✎	✎	/	3837	111
⚓	⚓	/	3847	1068

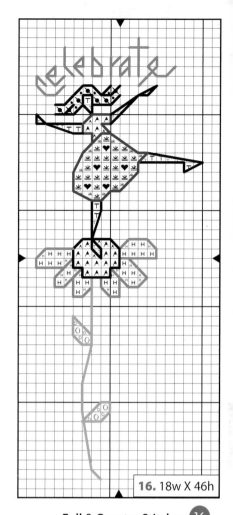

16. 18w X 46h

Full & Quarter Stitches 16

x	1/4	Back	DMC	Anc.
		/	335	38
○	○		472	253
♥			604	55
H	H		605	50
●	●		743	302
A	A		745	300
		/	921	1003
T	T		948	1011
⚹	⚹		964	185
		/	3347	266
		/	3812	188

5. 34w X 47h

Full & Quarter Stitches 15

x	1/4	Back	FK	DMC	Anc.
⊙				1	2
$				208	110
△				209	109
■		/	•	310	403
♥		/		666	46
⚓	⚓			826	161
2				970	316
H	H			977	1002
4				988	243
⧄				993	186
♣	♣			3345	268
#				3348	264
⊠				3755	140
a	a			3776	1048
⁂	⁂			3814	188
୭				3862	903

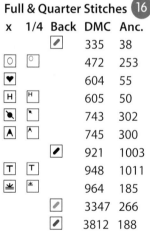

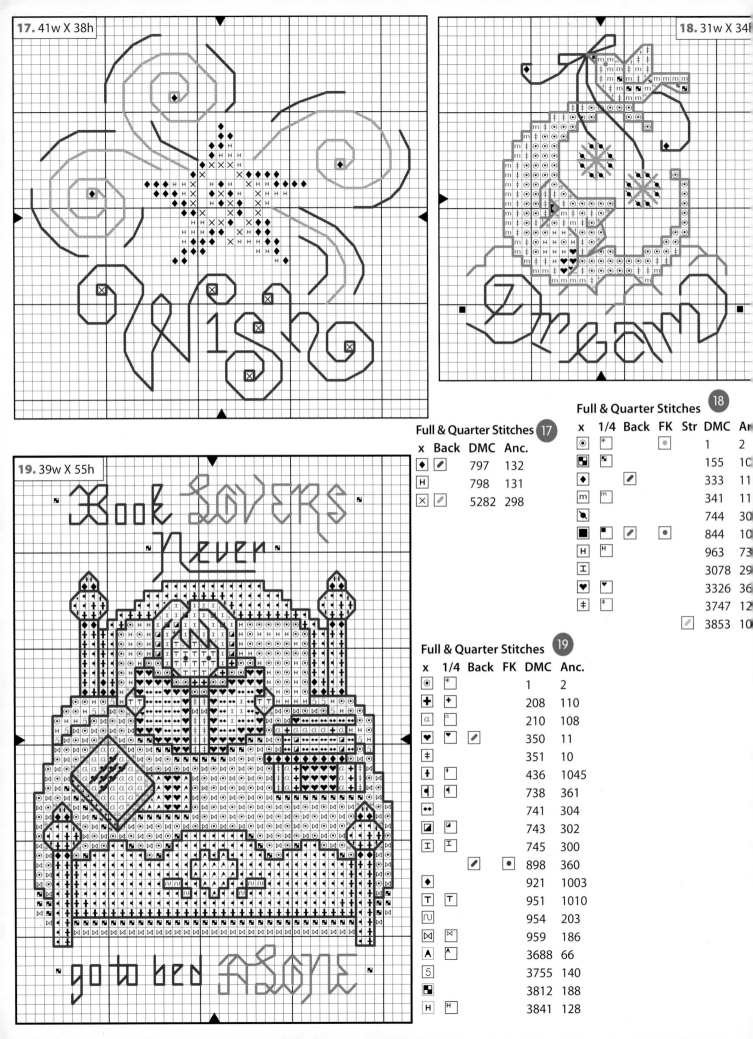

17. 41w X 38h

18. 31w X 34h

19. 39w X 55h

Full & Quarter Stitches ⑰

x	Back	DMC	Anc.
◆	✎	797	132
H		798	131
✕	✎	5282	298

Full & Quarter Stitches ⑱

x	1/4	Back	FK	Str	DMC	An
⊙	⊡			●	1	2
▣	▣				155	10
◆		✎			333	11
m	m				341	11
◥					744	30
■	■	✎	●		844	10
H	H				963	73
I					3078	29
♥	♥				3326	36
‡	‡				3747	12
	✎				3853	10

Full & Quarter Stitches ⑲

x	1/4	Back	FK	DMC	Anc.
⊙	⊡			1	2
✚	✚			208	110
a	a			210	108
♥	♥	✎		350	11
‡				351	10
✚				436	1045
◀	◀			738	361
✦				741	304
◩	◪			743	302
I	I			745	300
		✎	●	898	360
◆				921	1003
T	T			951	1010
U				954	203
⋈	⋈			959	186
A	A			3688	66
5				3755	140
▪				3812	188
H	H			3841	128

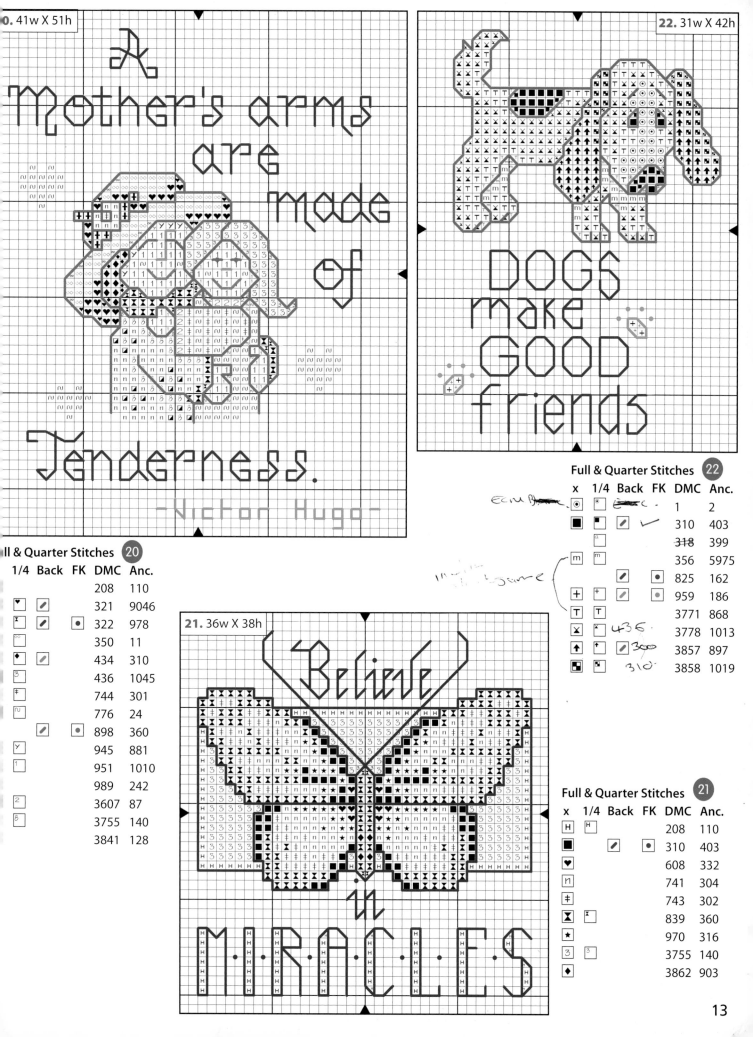

0. 41w X 51h

A
Mother's arms
are
made
of
Tenderness.
—Victor Hugo—

22. 31w X 42h

DOGS
make
GOOD
friends

21. 36w X 38h

Believe
in
M·I·R·A·C·L·E·S

Full & Quarter Stitches 22

x	1/4	Back	FK	DMC	Anc.
⊙	⊙			1	2
■	■	/	✓	310	403
				318	399
m	m			356	5975
		/	⊙	825	162
+	+	/	⊙	959	186
T	T			3771	868
X	X			3778	1013
↑	↑	/		3857	897
■	■			3858	1019

ll & Quarter Stitches 20

	1/4	Back	FK	DMC	Anc.
				208	110
♥		/		321	9046
X	X	/	⊙	322	978
	∞			350	11
♦		/		434	310
3				436	1045
‡				744	301
2				776	24
		/	⊙	898	360
Y				945	881
1				951	1010
				989	242
2				3607	87
ß				3755	140
				3841	128

Full & Quarter Stitches 21

x	1/4	Back	FK	DMC	Anc.
H	H			208	110
■		/	⊙	310	403
♥				608	332
n				741	304
‡				743	302
X	X			839	360
★				970	316
3	3			3755	140
♦				3862	903

13

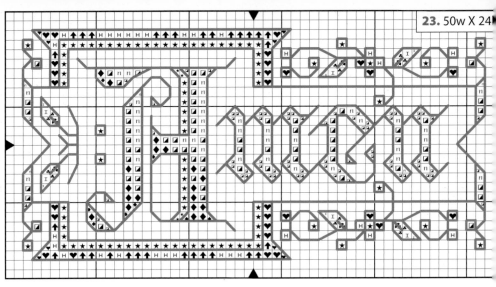

23. 50w X 24

Full & Quarter Stitches ㉓

x	1/4	Back	DMC	Anc.
I	I		471	266
◆	◆		797	132
◪	◪		798	131
n	n		799	136
		✎	801	359
♣	♣		3346	267
♥	♥		3350	59
↑			3731	76
H			3733	75
★	★		5282	298

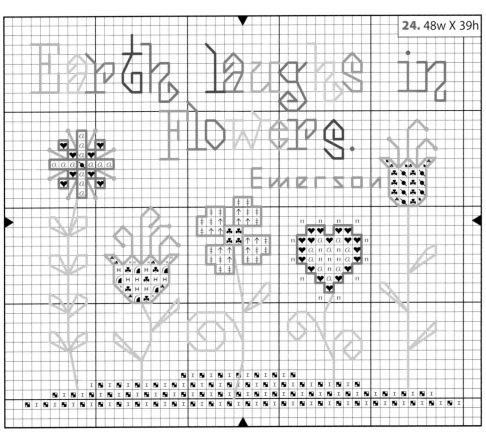

24. 48w X 39h

Full & Quarter Stitches ㉔

x	1/4	Back	FK	DMC	Anc.
		✎		322	978
↑		✎		340	118
a				351	10
♥		✎	●	666	46
◣	◩	✎	◉	741	304
♣	♣			742	303
H	H			744	301
n				963	73
		✎		3345	268
I				3347	266
◪				3348	264
◪		✎		3607	87
‡				3747	120

Full & Quarter Stitches ㉕

x	1/4	Back	FK	DMC	Anc.
↑		✎		797	132
m				798	131
◆				799	136
		✎		801	359
I				963	73
♥	♥	✎	●	3350	59
◪	◪			3731	76
A	A			3733	75
H				3747	120
⊙	⊙			5282	298

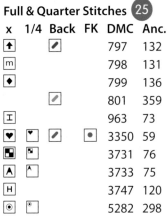

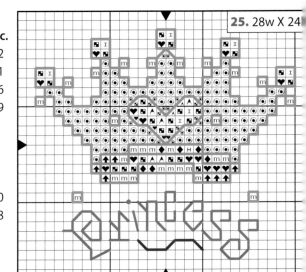

25. 28w X 24

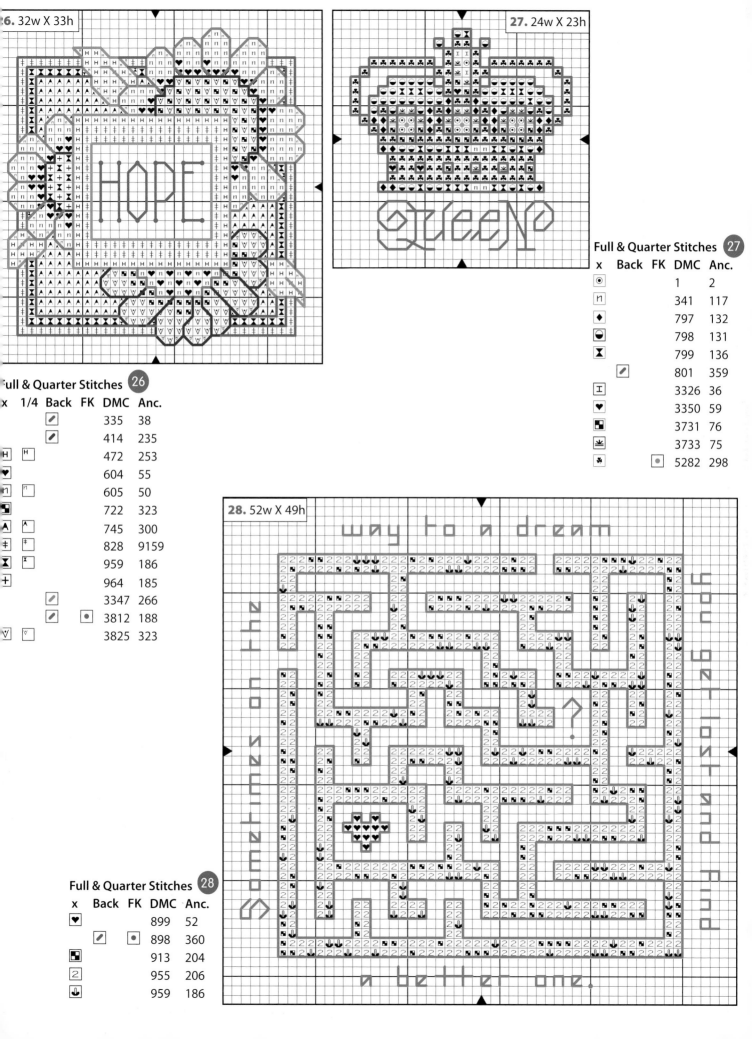

26. 32w X 33h

27. 24w X 23h

28. 52w X 49h

Full & Quarter Stitches 27

x	Back	FK	DMC	Anc.
◉			1	2
n			341	117
◆			797	132
◖			798	131
⊠			799	136
	✎		801	359
I			3326	36
♥			3350	59
▣			3731	76
✹			3733	75
✿		◉	5282	298

Full & Quarter Stitches 26

x	1/4	Back	FK	DMC	Anc.
		✎		335	38
		✎		414	235
H	H			472	253
♥				604	55
n	n			605	50
▣				722	323
▲	▲			745	300
‡	‡			828	9159
⊠	⊠			959	186
				964	185
		✎		3347	266
		✎	◉	3812	188
∨	∨			3825	323

Full & Quarter Stitches 28

x	Back	FK	DMC	Anc.
♥			899	52
	✎	◉	898	360
▣			913	204
2			955	206
⚓			959	186

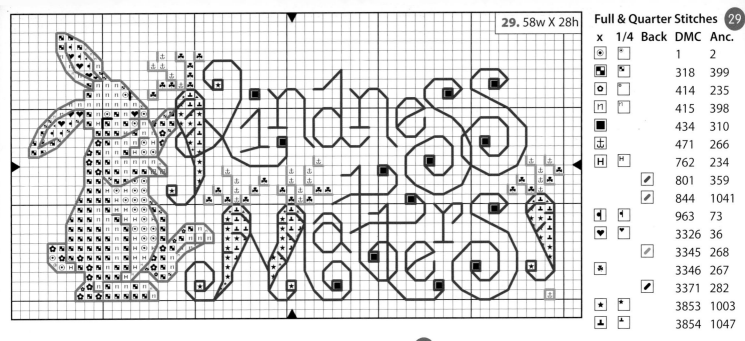

Full & Quarter Stitches 29

x	1/4	Back	DMC	Anc.
⊙	⊙		1	2
■	■		318	399
⊘	○		414	235
n	n		415	398
■			434	310
⚓			471	266
H	H		762	234
		✎	801	359
		✎	844	1041
◀	◀		963	73
♥	♥		3326	36
		✎	3345	268
❀			3346	267
		✎	3371	282
★	★		3853	1003
⚓	⚓		3854	1047

30. 25w X 56h

Full & Quarter Stitches 30

x	1/2	Back	FK	DMC	Anc.
		✎	⦁	801	359
	◹			963	73
+	+			3326	36
		✎	⦁	3350	59
♥				3733	75

Full & Quarter Stitches

x	1/4	Back	DMC	An.
♥			321	904
T	T		351	10
✖	✖		413	401
◪	◪		414	235
H	H		676	891
⏹	⏹		729	890
n	n		745	300
⚓			815	43
		✎	898	360

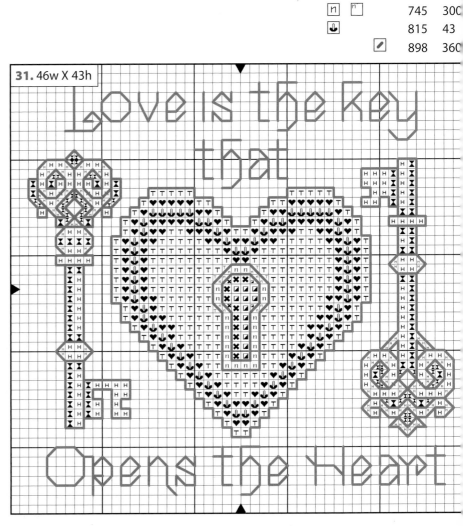

31. 46w X 43h

Full & Quarter Stitches 32

x	Back	FK	DMC	Anc.
⊙			1	2
H			155	109
↑	✎		333	119
◪			744	301
■	✎	•	844	1041
‡			963	73
2			3078	292
⌘			3326	36
◆			3350	59
✣			3731	76
◣			3733	75

32. 57w X 41h

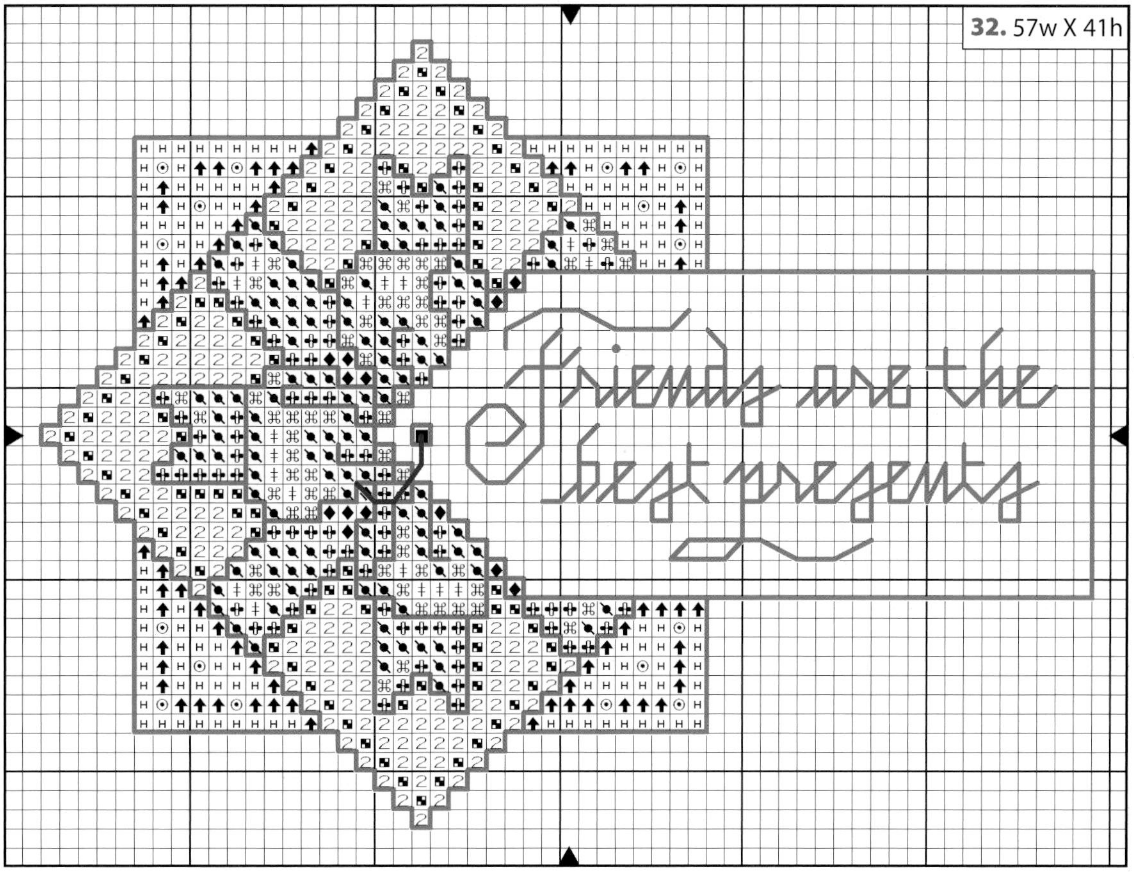

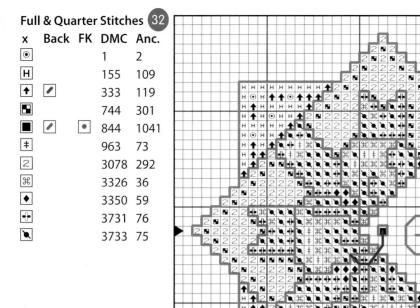

33. 41w X 20h

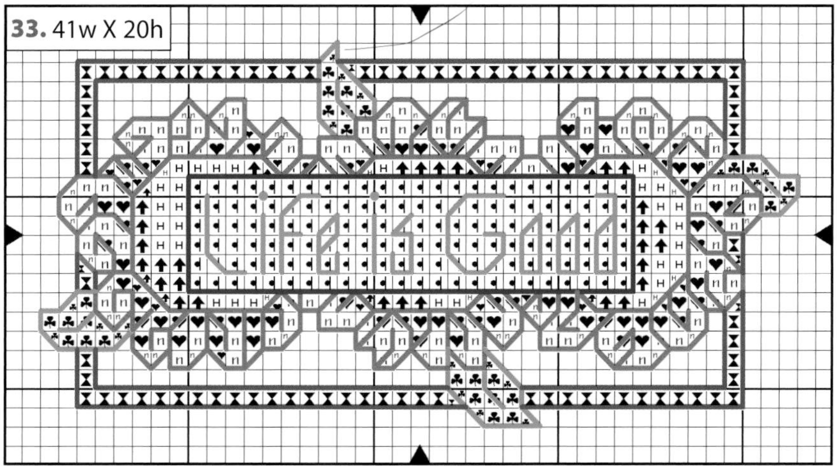

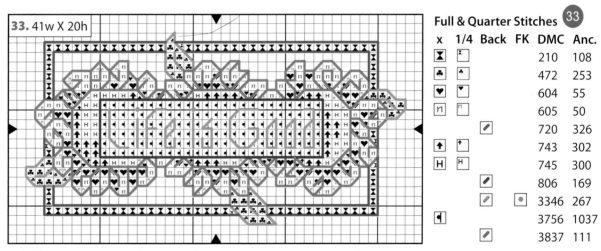

Full & Quarter Stitches 33

x	1/4	Back	FK	DMC	Anc.
⧗	⧗			210	108
♣	♣			472	253
♥	♥			604	55
∩	∩			605	50
		✎		720	326
↑	↑			743	302
H	H			745	300
		✎		806	169
		✎	•	3346	267
◖				3756	1037
		✎		3837	111

Full & Quarter Stitches 34

x	Back	FK	DMC	Anc.
∩			318	399
◪			414	235
✚			743	302
‡			744	301
◆			844	1041
↑			921	1003
■	✎	•	3371	382
$			3853	1003
∾			3854	1047

34. 27w X 28h

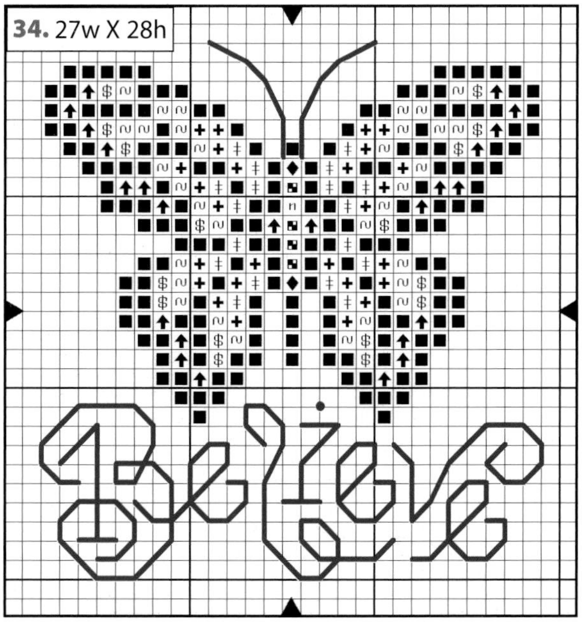

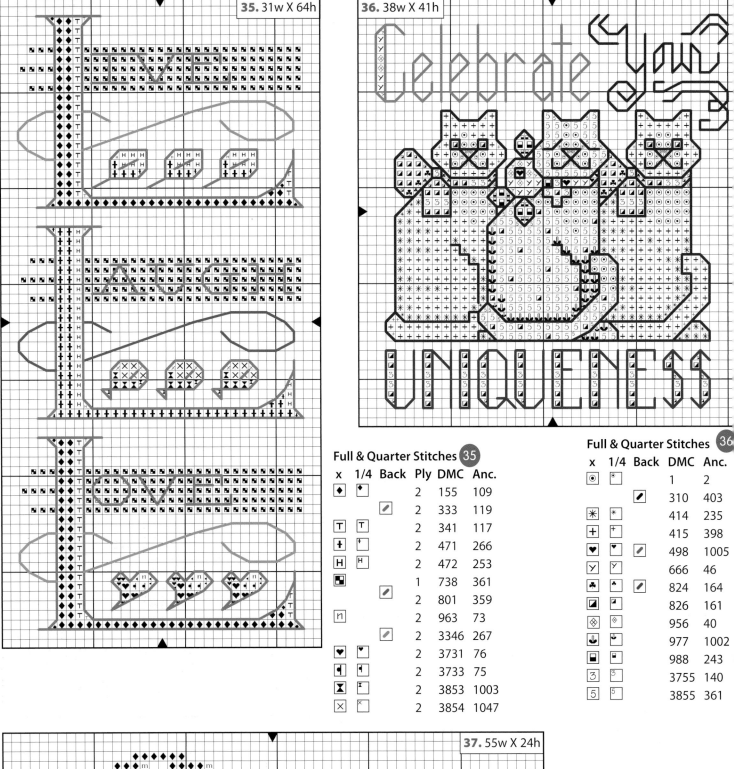

35. 31w X 64h

36. 38w X 41h

Full & Quarter Stitches 35

x	1/4	Back	Ply	DMC	Anc.
◆	◆		2	155	109
		✎	2	333	119
			2	341	117
T	T		2	471	266
✚	✚		2	472	253
H	H		2	738	361
■			1	738	361
		✎	2	801	359
n			2	963	73
		✎	2	3346	267
♥	♥		2	3731	76
◀	◀		2	3733	75
✗	✗		2	3853	1003
✕	✕		2	3854	1047

Full & Quarter Stitches 36

x	1/4	Back	DMC	Anc.
⊙	⊡		1	2
		✎	310	403
✳	✳		414	235
✚	✚		415	398
♥	♥	✎	498	1005
Y	Y		666	46
♣	♣	✎	824	164
◪	◪		826	161
⊗	⊗		956	40
⚓	⚓		977	1002
▣	▣		988	243
3	3		3755	140
5	5		3855	361

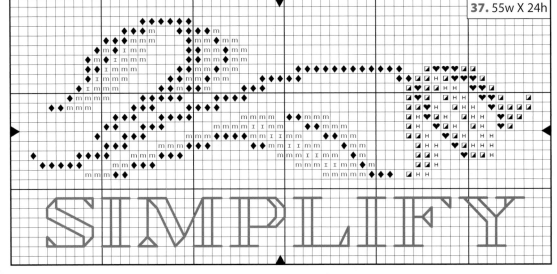

37. 55w X 24h

Full & Quarter Stitches 37

x	Back	DMC	Anc.
◆		501	878
m		502	877
I		503	876
	✎	801	359
♥		3350	59
◪		3731	76
H		3733	75

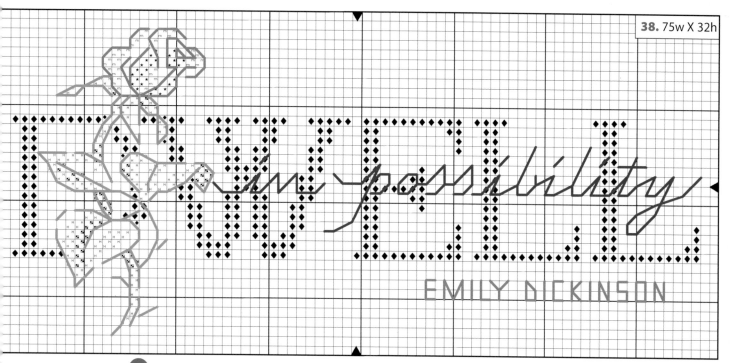

EMILY DICKINSON

Full & Quarter Stitches 38

x	1/4	1/2	Back	DMC	Anc.
▨	▨	▨		471	266
H	H	H		472	253
◆	◆			503	876
			✎	801	359
m	m	m		3326	36
			✎	3345	368
			✎	3350	59
★	★	★		3733	75

Full & Quarter Stitches 39

x		Back	DMC	Anc.
✿			501	878
⊙			502	877
		✎	801	359
♥			3350	59
▦			3731	76
H			3733	75
⁞			5282	298

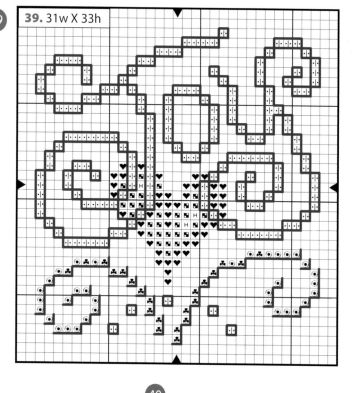

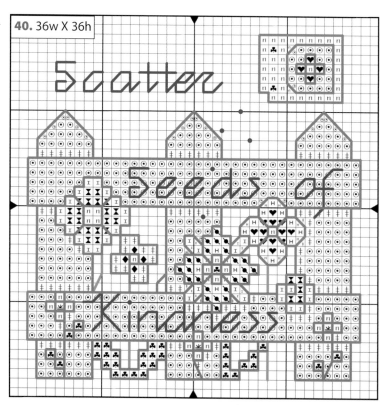

Scatter

Full & Quarter Stitches 40

x	1/4	Back	FK	DMC	Anc.
⊙	□			1	2
▣		✎	●	208	110
I	I			211	342
♥			●	321	9046
✹				721	324
n	n			744	301
H	H			776	24
◣				899	52
		✎		938	381
♣		✎		989	242
◆				3838	118
‡	‡			3840	120

19

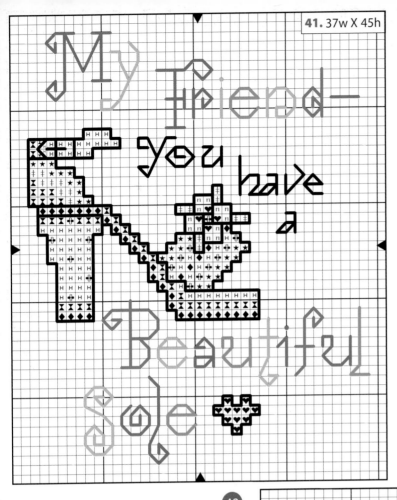

My Friend—
you have a
Beautiful
Sole

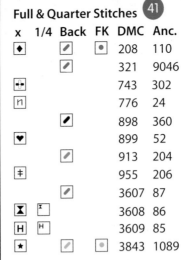

Full & Quarter Stitches 41

x	1/4	Back	FK	DMC	Anc.
◆		✎	⊙	208	110
		✎		321	9046
⊹				743	302
n				776	24
		✎		898	360
♥				899	52
		✎		913	204
‡				955	206
		✎		3607	87
✕	✕			3608	86
H	H			3609	85
★		✎	⊙	3843	1089

Full & Quarter Stitches 42

x	1/4	Back	FK	DMC	Anc.
⊙	⊙			1	2
◣	◣			208	110
		✎		322	978
⊕	⊕			434	310
★	★	✎		742	303
$				743	302
1				776	24
■	■	✎	⊙	898	360
n	n			945	881
∾				954	203
◆				959	186
✕				3608	86
T				3609	85
‡	‡			3761	928
◼				3841	128
⚓				3845	1089

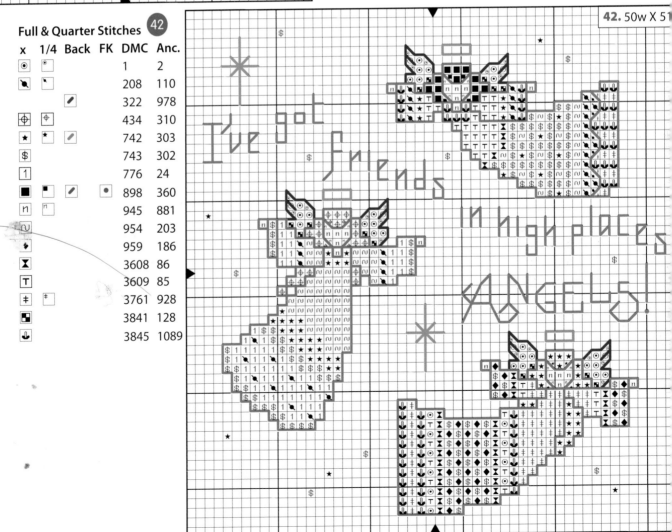

I've got Friends in high places ANGELS!

20

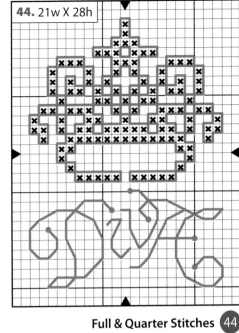

Full & Quarter Stitches 44

x	Back	FK	DMC	Anc.
	✐	●	801	359
✖			5282	298

Full & Quarter Stitches 43

	1/4	Back	FK	DMC	Anc.
				209	109
				211	342
				310	403
			♥	321	9046
				605	50
				741	304
				743	302
				745	300
		✐		895	1044
		✐		938	381
				946	332
				956	40
				989	242
		✐	●	3807	122
				3838	118
				3839	140
				3840	120

Full & Quarter Stitches 45

x	1/4	Back	FK	DMC	Anc.
◆		✐		322	978
n				340	118
◨				351	10
★				563	208
♥		✐	●	666	46
		✐	●	741	304
4	4			742	303
Y	Y			744	301
I				963	73
		✐		3345	268
‡	⊦			3348	264
C				3747	120
+				3833	1023
⋈				3841	128

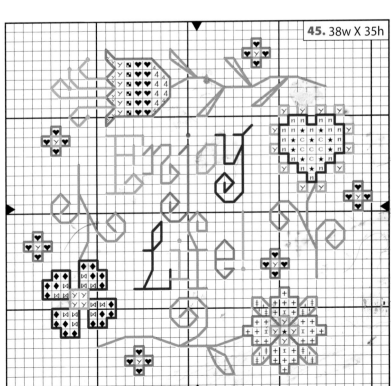

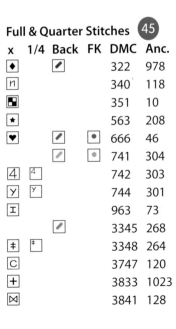

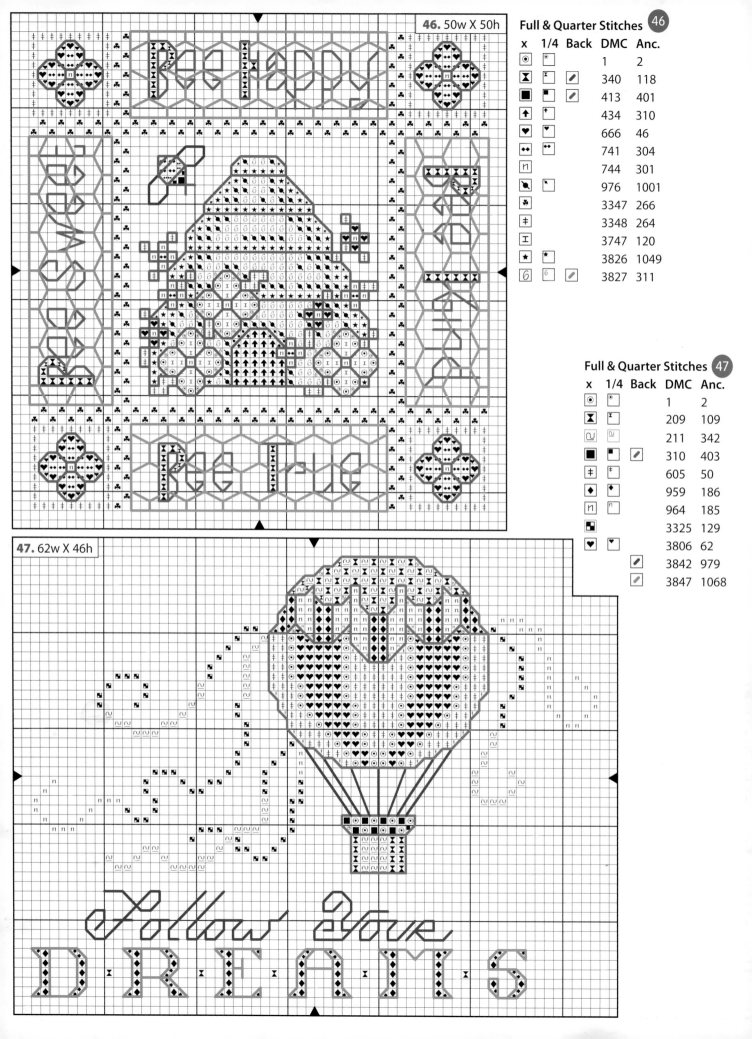

46. 50w X 50h

46

Full & Quarter Stitches 46

x	1/4	Back	DMC	Anc.
⊙	⊡		1	2
☒	⊠	✎	340	118
■	◧	✎	413	401
↑	↑		434	310
♥	♥		666	46
◆◆	◆◆		741	304
n	n		744	301
◨	◺		976	1001
♣			3347	266
‡			3348	264
I			3747	120
★	★		3826	1049
6	6	✎	3827	311

Full & Quarter Stitches 47

x	1/4	Back	DMC	Anc.
⊙	⊡		1	2
☒	⊠		209	109
∾	∾		211	342
■	◧	✎	310	403
‡	‡		605	50
◆	◆		959	186
n	n		964	185
◪			3325	129
♥	♥		3806	62
		✎	3842	979
		✎	3847	1068

47. 62w X 46h

Full & Quarter Stitches (48)

x	1/4	Back	FK	DMC	Anc.
↑	↑			155	109
H	H			341	117
◆	◆			471	266
⋂	⋂			472	253
⋈	⋈			554	96
I	I			738	361
		✎	●	801	359
		✎	●	820	134
+				963	73
♥	♥			3731	76
‡	‡			3733	75
★	★			3853	1003
⟩	⟩			3854	1047

48. 50w X 65h

49. 53w X 31h

DARE TO BE DIFFERENT

Full & Quarter Stitches (49)

x	1/4	Back	DMC	Anc.
◉			1	2
◆		✎	208	110
⋂	⋂		209	109
■	■	✎	310	403
+	+		351	10
♥	♥		498	1005
$	$		666	46
↑	↑		824	164
2		✎	826	161
⊟	⊟		977	1002
3	3		988	243
⊠	⊡		3345	268
⋈	⋈		3348	264
T	T		3755	140
1	1		3855	361

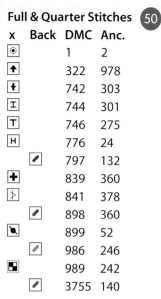

Full & Quarter Stitches   50

x	Back	DMC	Anc.
⊙		1	2
⬆		322	978
⊹		742	303
I		744	301
T		746	275
H		776	24
	✎	797	132
✚		839	360
▸		841	378
	✎	898	360
◣		899	52
	✎	986	246
◪		989	242
	✎	3755	140

Full & Quarter Stitches   51

x	1/4	Back	FK	DMC	Anc.
⊙				1	2
◆	◆			208	110
◖	◗			209	109
■	◼	✎		310	403
⊹	⊹			353	6
♥	♥	✎		666	46
✖	✕		⊙	824	164
✖	✖			826	161
4	4			956	40
⊹	⊹			977	1002
♣	♣			988	243
m	m			3348	264
7				3755	140
★	★			3771	868
H	H			3855	361

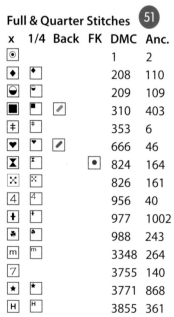

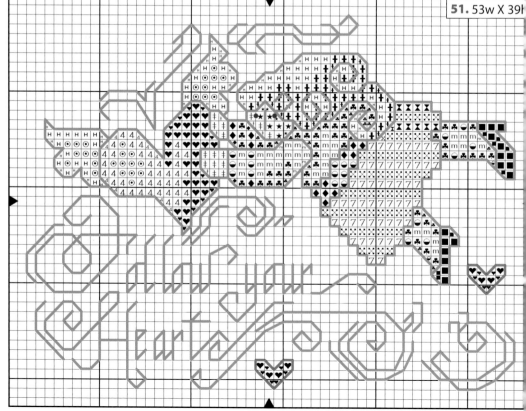

Full & Quarter Stitches 52

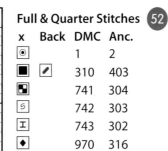

x		Back	DMC	Anc.
⊙			1	2
■	✎		310	403
◨			741	304
s			742	303
I			743	302
◆			970	316
a			3755	140

Full & Quarter Stitches 53

x	1/4	Back	FK	DMC	Anc.
◨				208	110
+	+			210	108
‡				211	342
		✎	●	312	979
↑	↑			322	978
%				351	10
♥				606	334
◆				742	303
H				744	301
⋒				772	259
		✎		898	360
+		✎		989	242
✕				3687	68
◖				3688	66
⋒				3689	49
m	m			3755	140
I	I			3841	128

If friends were flowers I'd pick you

54. 62w X 68h

Full & Quarter Stitches (54)

x	1/4	Back	FK	DMC	Anc.
H	H			153	95
m	m			209	109
♥	♥			304	1006
■	■	/		310	403
✕	✕	/		355	1014
✕	✕			402	1047
↑				602	63
✕				603	62
⌒				604	55
I				605	50
T	T			951	1010
●	●			3801	35
◆	◆	/	●	3837	111
★				3853	1003
◈	◈			3856	367

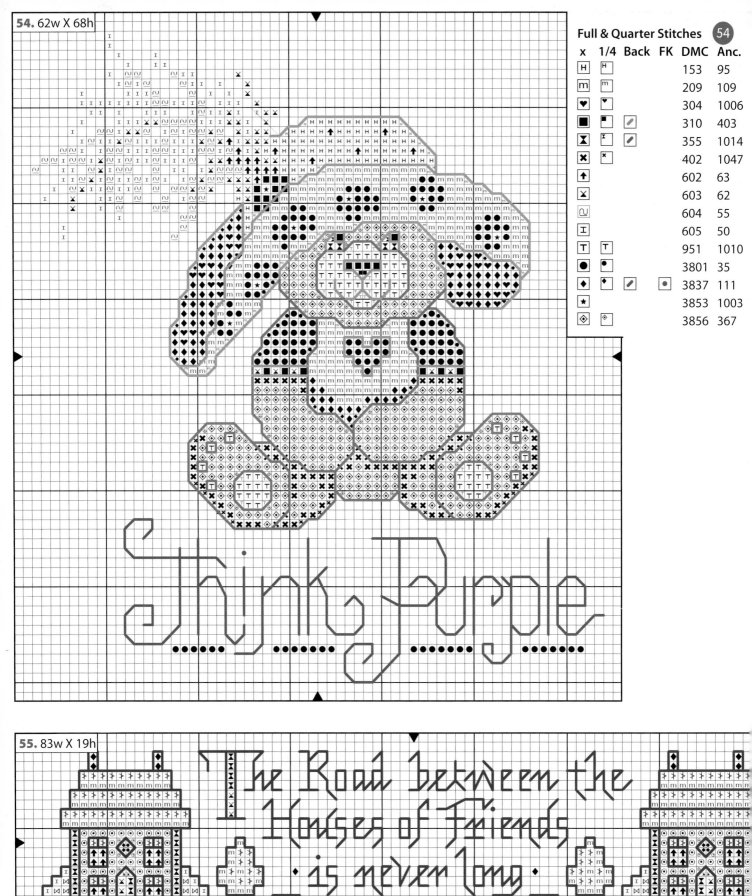

55. 83w X 19h

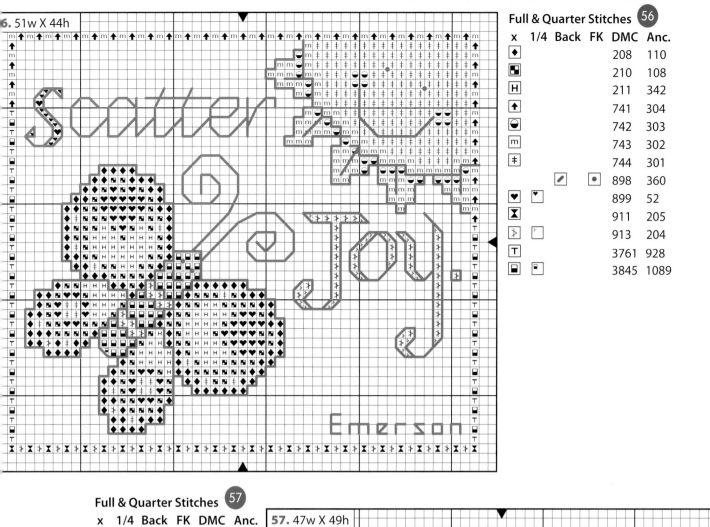

6. 51w X 44h

Full & Quarter Stitches 56

x	1/4	Back	FK	DMC	Anc.
◆				208	110
▣				210	108
H				211	342
↑				741	304
◗				742	303
m				743	302
‡				744	301
		✏	●	898	360
♥	♥			899	52
⊠				911	205
⋟		▷		913	204
T				3761	928
▣	▪			3845	1089

Full & Quarter Stitches 57

x	1/4	Back	FK	DMC	Anc.
◆	◆			208	110
m	m			210	108
H				211	342
		✏		317	400
♥		✏		350	11
T	T			776	24
↑	↑			798	131
▣	▫			813	161
✷	✷			899	52
⊙		✏		913	204
I				955	206

Full & Quarter Stitches 55

x	1/4	Back	FK	DMC	Anc.
⊙	⊡			1	2
⊺				471	266
↑				744	301
◆	◆	✏	●	797	132
⊠	˟			798	131
⊠				799	136
n				3078	292
▣				3345	268
⊠				3346	267
✿				3826	1049
m				3853	1003
▷				3854	1047

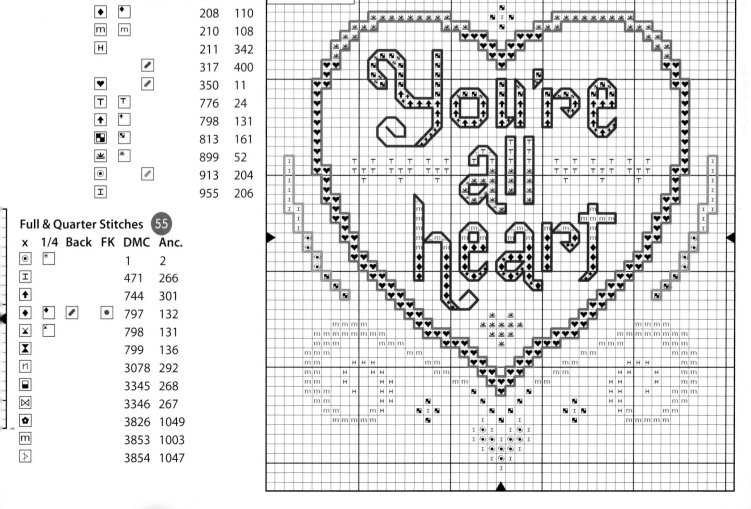

57. 47w X 49h

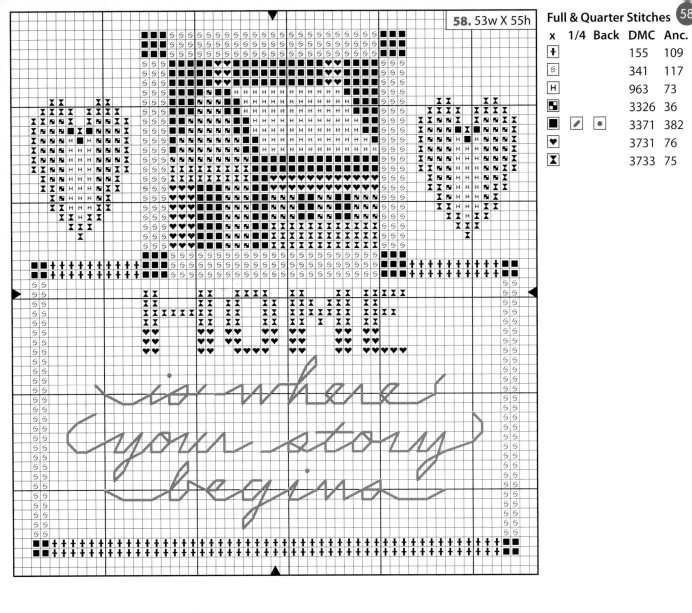

58. 53w X 55h

Full & Quarter Stitches 58

x	1/4	Back	DMC	Anc.
✚			155	109
⑤			341	117
H			963	73
◨			3326	36
■	╱	•	3371	382
♥			3731	76
✕			3733	75

Full & Quarter Stitches 59

x	Back	DMC	Anc.
✖ ╱		333	119

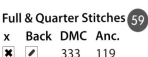

59. 67w X 31h

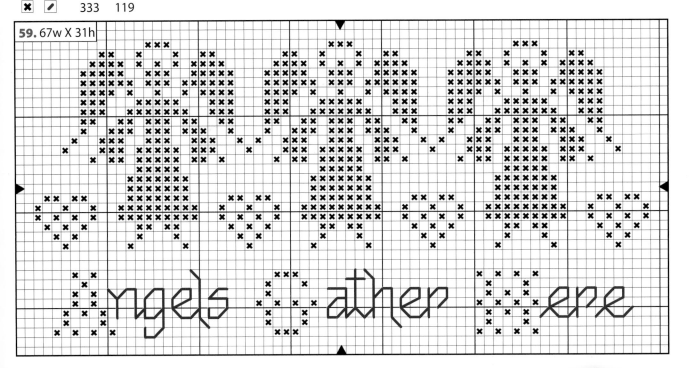

Full & Quarter Stitches 60

60. 49w X 49h

x	1/4	Back	FK	DMC	Anc.
⊙				1	2
♥	♥	✎		321	9046
Z				402	1047
⊠				434	310
T				437	362
△				721	324
⋈				739	387
1	1			746	275
H				776	24
↑	↑	✎	●	898	360
◀				899	52
◆				911	205
5				913	204
▣				3746	1030

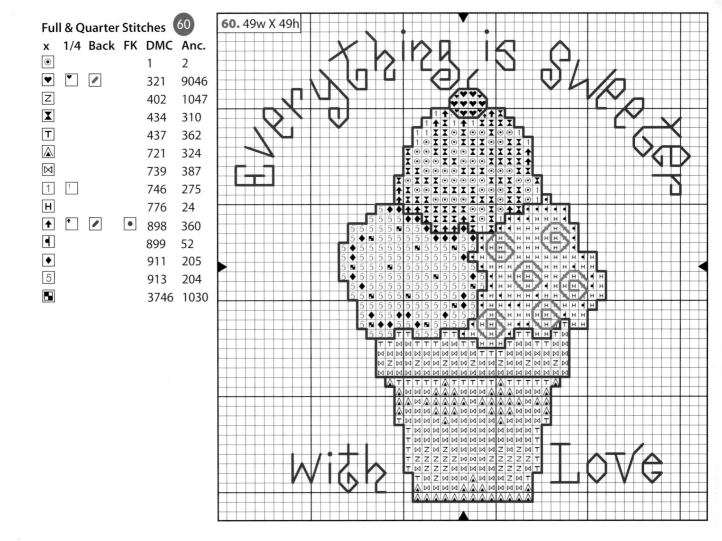

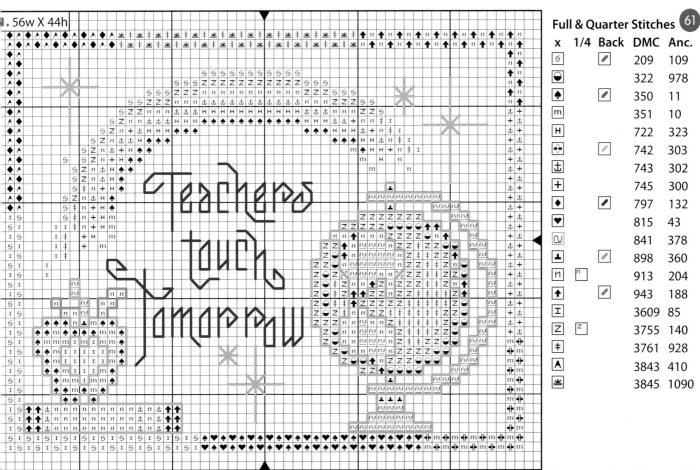

Full & Quarter Stitches 61

x	1/4	Back	DMC	Anc.
S		✎	209	109
◑			322	978
♠		✎	350	11
m			351	10
H			722	323
✛		✎	742	303
⊥			743	302
+			745	300
◆		✎	797	132
♥			815	43
∾			841	378
⊥		✎	898	360
n	n		913	204
↑		✎	943	188
I			3609	85
Z	z		3755	140
‡			3761	928
A			3843	410
⬇			3845	1090

29

The best things in life are God, friends and a hot cup of coffee!

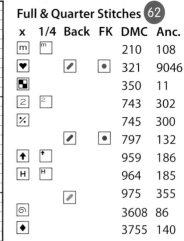

x	1/4	Back	FK	DMC	Anc.
m	m			210	108
❤		✐	●	321	9046
◼				350	11
2	2			743	302
⅍				745	300
		✐	●	797	132
↑	↑			959	186
H	H			964	185
		✐		975	355
◉				3608	86
◆				3755	140

x	1/4	Back	FK	DMC	Anc.
⊙	⊙			1	2
⊥	⊥			210	108
		✐	●	312	979
		✐		322	978
♠	♠			436	1045
‡	‡			745	300
I	I			776	24
		✐		898	360
❤	❤			899	52
		✐	●	910	229
✚	✚			913	204
H	H			951	1010
n	n			955	206
⊻	⊻			964	185
◆	◆		●	3607	87
⟩	⟩			3608	86
T	T			3756	1037

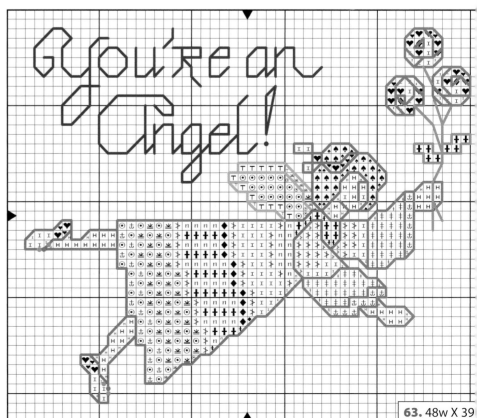

You're an Angel!

64. 54w X 54h

x	1/4	Back	DMC	Anc.
☒	☒		208	110
		✎	312	979
▲	▲		958	187
H	H		3688	66
		✎	3803	972
I	I		3807	122

Full & Quarter Stitches ⓺⓹

x	Back	FK	DMC	Anc.
	✎		743	302
◆	✎	●	792	941
▣			793	176
m			794	175
H			3747	120

65. 70w X 39h

66. 41w X 49h

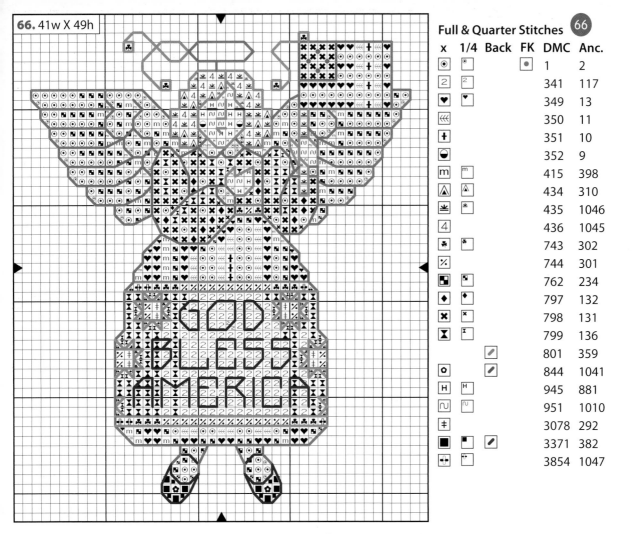

Full & Quarter Stitches 66

x	1/4	Back	FK	DMC	Anc.
⊙	⊡		●	1	2
2	2			341	117
♥	♥			349	13
⫷				350	11
✝				351	10
◖				352	9
m	m			415	398
▲	▲			434	310
⚘	⚘			435	1046
4				436	1045
♣	♣			743	302
%				744	301
▣	▣			762	234
◆	◆			797	132
✕	✕			798	131
✕	✕			799	136
			✎	801	359
◉			✎	844	1041
H	H			945	881
∿	∿			951	1010
‡				3078	292
■	■		✎	3371	382
⊞	⊞			3854	1047

Full & Quarter Stitches 67

x	1/4	Back	Str	DMC	Anc.
⊙	⊙			1	2
◆	◆			208	110
n	n			209	109
■			✎	310	403
T	T			402	1047
♣	♣		✎	701	227
2				703	238
‡	‡			762	234
⊎				824	164
△				826	161
⋔	⋔			956	40
⊠	⊠			970	316
H				3755	140

67. 39w X 46h

Full & Quarter Stitches 68

x	Back	FK	DMC	Anc.
↑			208	110
⊠			322	978
★			502	877
♥			600	59
⧊			601	57
m			603	62
I			605	50
✝			741	304
✕			742	303
‡			743	302
T			744	301
H			775	128
	✎	●	938	381
▣			987	244
✛			989	242
◪			3325	129

68. 46w X 58h

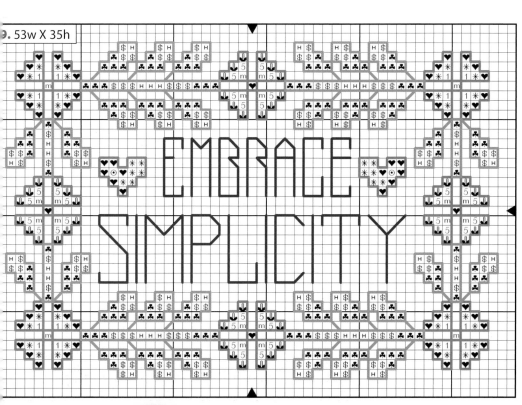

9. 53w X 35h

Full & Quarter Stitches 69

x	Back	DMC	Anc.
⊙		1	2
♥	✎	666	46
5		741	304
m		743	302
	✎	824	164
✳		956	40
⬇		970	316
$		988	243
♣	✎	3345	268
H		3348	264
1		3708	31

70

Full & Quarter Stitches (70)

x	1/4	Back	FK	DMC	Anc.
⊙	⊡			1	2
◆	◆			208	110
m				210	108
‡				211	342
↑	↑	✎	●	434	310
★	★			436	1045
∿	∿			676	891
1	1			677	886
✚	✚			721	324
T	T			722	323
◑	◑			738	361
5	5			776	24
✚	✚			818	23
		✎	●	825	162
▲				826	161
■	■	✎	●	898	360
♥	♥			899	52
♣	♣			913	204
I	I			951	1010
?	?			955	206

70. 47w X 52h

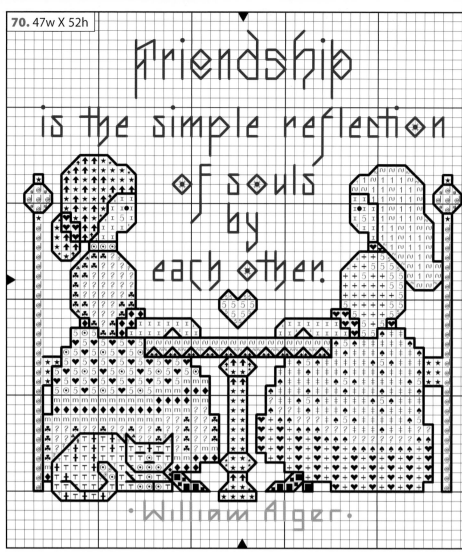

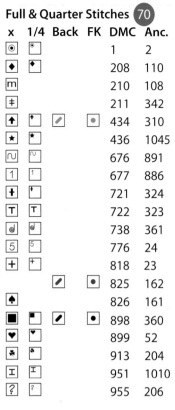

71

71. 55w X 39h

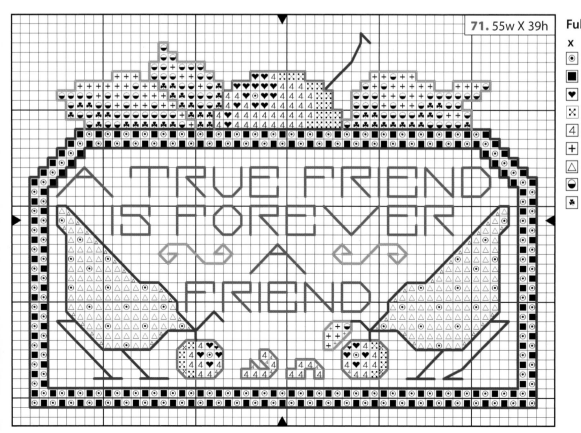

Full & Quarter Stitches (71)

x	1/4	Back	DMC	Anc.
⊙			1	2
■		✎	310	403
♥	♥	✎	498	1005
⊠	⊠		608	332
4	4		666	46
✚	✚		993	186
△	△		3755	140
◑		✎	3814	188
✿		✎	3847	1068
			3837	111

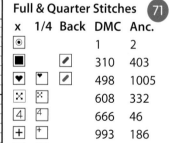

Full & Quarter Stitches 72

x	1/4	Back	FK	DMC	Anc.
↑				434	310
T	T			436	1045
■		✎	●	839	360
√	√			841	378
✿				890	218
⊙				987	244
m				989	242
H				3348	264

72. 50w X 45h

Mighty Oaks from Tiny Acorns Grow.

73. 50w X 50h

At one glance I love you with a thousand hearts

Full & Quarter Stitches 73

x	1/4	Back	FK	DMC	Anc.
m				209	109
♥				347	1025
◣	◪			351	10
		✎		414	235
		✎	●	798	131
♦				809	130
✕				3688	66
‡				3689	49
■	◪			3821	305
		✎		5282	298

Full & Quarter Stitches (74)

x	1/4	Back	FK	DMC	Anc.
◼	◻	✎		155	109
H	H			164	240
a				210	108
		✎	●	312	979
		✎	●	317	400
◼	◼	✎		434	310
◤	◤			436	1045
n	n			738	361
◆	◆			742	303
▣	▣			743	302
‡	‡			745	300
3			●	964	185
♣	♣	✎		987	244
◭	◭			989	242
◼				3688	66
⊥	⊥			3689	49
↑	↑			3755	140
T	T			3756	1037
Z	z			3841	128

Full & Quarter Stitches (75)

x	1/4	Back	FK	DMC	Anc.
I				341	117
◼				471	266
T				472	253
m				743	302
‡				744	301
	◼	✎	●	797	132
⊥				798	131
◼				799	136
H				3078	292
◆				3346	267
↑			●	3854	1047

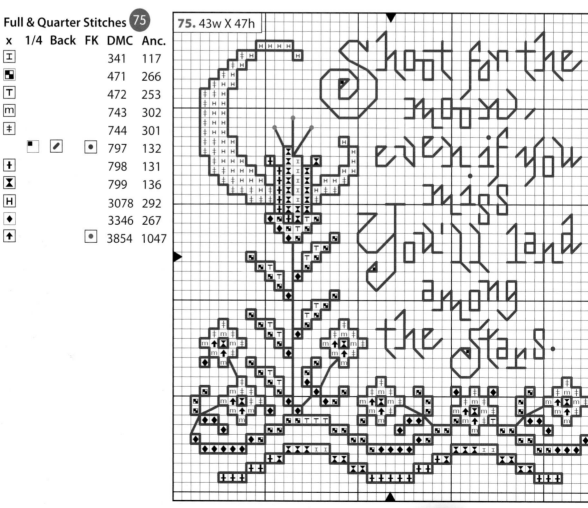